The Painted Garden

MILNER CRAFT SERIES

The Painted Garden

DESIGNS FOR FOLK ART AND TOLE PAINTING

KATE COOMBE

SALLY MILNER PUBLISHING

First published in 1992 by
Sally Milner Publishing Pty Ltd
P.O. Box 2104
Bowral NSW 2576
Australia

Reprinted 1992, 1993 (twice), 1994, 1999

© Kate Coombe, 1992

Concept design by David Constable
Layout by Gatya Kelly, Doric Order
Photography by John Knight
Typeset in Australia by Asset Typesetting Pty Ltd
Printed in Malaysia by SRM Production Services

National Library of Australia
Cataloguing-in-Publication data:

Coombe, Kate
    The painted garden.

    ISBN 1 86351 236 5.

    1. Garden ornaments and furniture. 2. Decoration and
    ornament – Plant forms. I. Title.
    (Series: Milner craft series)

749.8

CONTENTS

ACKNOWLEDGEMENTS

I would like to dedicate this book to my very first art teacher, Mother Evangeline, who developed in me the total enjoyment of being creative. It was her enthusiasm for her subject and her students that inspired me to become an art teacher myself. Of course, the production of this book was also made possible by the support of my husband and daughters and the encouragement of friends.

SUPPLIES AND MATERIALS

If you are interested in any of the items or supplies appearing in this book, please send your request and a stamped self-addressed envelope to:

Folk Artifacts,
c/o Post Office
Gundaroo NSW 2620
Australia

FOREWORD

Decorative painting is now very popular in Australia, so I decided to put together this book to combine two of my favourite pastimes — painting and gardening. I actually paint better than I garden, but that is probably because I spend more time painting. My system for creating a wild cottage garden is expensive but eventually effective. As a plant dies, I keep replacing it with a different one until I find something that will live in that spot. Of course I have the greatest success with roses because they are wonderfully sturdy, although my brand of loving inattention has been able to wipe out quite a few.

I am hoping that because our garden is now graced by a painted terracotta bird feeder, a bird house, a wheelbarrow and painted pots, and I have a painted apron, garden tools and gloves, I might feel constrained to spend more time in my neglected area of ferns, flowers and phalaris!

When you are a painter, there comes a time when the house is full of decorative pieces, so you look further afield — to move outdoors and start painting in the garden is a logical step! I hope, too, that some of the patterns in this book will be useful to painters who would like to paint presents for the gardening people in their lives. I have only touched on a few of the ideas for painted decoration in the garden — there are still painted outdoor table mats, outdoor benches, mail boxes, house signs, plant labels, barbeque tools, and spades, forks and shovels, to name but a few.

I hope you enjoy using these patterns and that many gardens will be painted.

Kate Coombe

GETTING STARTED

The general steps for reproducing the paintings in this book are as follows. Prepare your item according to the surface instructions, including base coating, trace the pattern of your choice and apply it to your piece, then proceed to follow the instructions as directed for the individual painting.

The pieces I have painted for this book have been a mixture of 'found' metal and wooden items that I have picked up from old sheds, from clearing sales, and from second hand shops. I have also painted some new wooden pieces.

PREPARATION OF DIFFERENT SURFACES

There are several metal pieces in this book as well as wood and terracotta. Each surface needs a different preparation. The following steps are the ones I use most often.

METAL

If the metal is old and rusty I find it is worthwhile spending an extra $10 or $20 to have it sandblasted and primed before I base coat it in my chosen colour in flat enamel paint. The hours you would spend with a wire brush and rust-proof paint could be spent painting! It has also been my experience that the best base coat for metal is flat enamel paint. Acrylic base coat applied straight onto the metal tends to lift at the slightest knock. Even enamel base coat is very fragile until it is decorated and varnished. The easiest paint to use is the aerosol flat enamel. It is expensive if you do a great many metal pieces and not environmentally very sound if you cannot obtain the right aerosol, but if you are only going to be doing the odd piece it certainly saves on turps and brushes.

If the metal is new, check it carefully. On some galvanised metal the galvanising process can leave a faint greasy residue that will not accept any base coat. This has to be cleaned off first with vinegar, then the metal piece painted with Jo Sonja All Purpose Sealer and dried in the oven at 200°F (90°C) for ten minutes. Then you can base coat the metal with the enamel paint.

TERRACOTTA

Most terracotta pots are once-fired earthenware, which is porous — that is, it absorbs and retains water for a certain length of time. It is this quality that makes terracotta ideal for soil and plants, but not very good for layers of decorative paint. If you wish to decorate the porous clay pot, it must be sealed inside *and* outside. If it is only sealed on the outside, the moisture in the soil will push the decoration off the pot, and if only the inside is sealed then the water in the paint will be sucked into the clay, causing the brush to drag and make stroke work difficult. Jo Sonja All Purpose Sealer is particularly good because it doesn't make the surface too shiny. I also use the Jo Sonja All Purpose Sealer as a varnish for terracotta because of its durability.

WOOD

Raw wood needs to be sealed and base coated. The easiest way to do this is to combine Jo Sonja All Purpose Sealer with the base coat colour and paint onto the wood with two coats, sanding between each coat. Another advantage of sealer in the base coat is that you can handle the base-coated piece without it absorbing any moisture or grease off your hands.

DRYING TIMES

Before you can add another layer of paint over your first coat of acrylic, there is a brief pause needed. If you attempt a second coat too soon the original layer will pull up or streak.

When you have finished a piece, it is possible to varnish as soon as it is touch dry, but it is much better to allow a few days CURING time for the paint before you varnish.

GENERAL SUPPLIES

PAINT

I have used Jo Sonja Artist's Colours in this book and have found them excellent. For those of you who have access to, or prefer, bottled or other brands of acrylic paint, I have provided a colour conversion chart at the back of the book. Those interested in acquiring Jo Sonja Artist's Colours can contact the following suppliers:

Australia
Chroma Acrylics (NSW) Pty Ltd
Mt Ku-ring-gai, New South Wales
(02) 457 9922
(008) 02 3935

USA
Chroma Acrylics Inc
Hainesport, New Jersey
(609) 261 8500

UK
Thomas Seth & Company
Hartley, Kent
(474) 70 5077

NZ
Draw Art Supplies
Auckland, New Zealand
966 4862

Although it may seem that I ask you to mix quite a number of colours, I feel this is easier and more economical than referring to a vast range of various colours in a number of brands. You might notice I sometimes refer to Titanium White and Warm White. If I am specific and state the colour, it means that particular shade is best, but if I just refer to White, it means you may use either Warm White or Titanium White.

BRUSHES

The brushes you use are very important and are probably the most expensive item in your whole kit of supplies. I use a 1" (25 mm) synthetic brush for all base coating and varnishing. For stroke work and decorating I use a No. 2 or No. 3 and a No. 5 round synthetic brush, a No. 4 and a No. 8 flat brush and a No. 00 Long Liner. A clean, well-cared-for brush will last longer and give you better strokes with less effort than a brush with dried paint in it. It is most important to be very particular about always washing the paint out of the brush totally — either between colours or between painting stints. It is also a sensible economy to work some brush cleaner or detergent into your brush after you have finished a painting session and before you give your brushes a final wash.

MISCELLANEOUS SUPPLIES

Other items besides brushes and paints that will be useful to you will be:
a stylus
transfer paper (light and dark)
tracing paper
medium and fine sandpaper
Jo Sonja All Purpose Sealer
Jo Sonja Retarder and Antiquing Medium
Jo Sonja Glaze Medium
a hair dryer
paper towel

TERMS AND TECHNIQUES
OF FOLK ART

LOAD THE BRUSH

This means putting paint on the brush!

SIDELOAD

Once you have loaded the main colour into the brush, touch one side of the point of the bristles into the edge of the side load colour. You should end up with a 'fingernail' of extra colour on the tip of one side of your brush. Keep this colour uppermost on your brush if you want it to appear at the beginning of your stroke or underneath your brush if you wish this colour to appear at the end of the stroke.

DOUBLE LOAD

Load your brush with one colour, then poke the tip of the bristles into the second colour and paint your stroke. The second colour will appear the strongest and a blending with the original colour in the brush will appear at the end of the stroke.

BASE COAT

This refers to painting the object or an area of the design with a smooth even coverage so that it becomes an opaque single colour. Allow this to dry completely (unless the instructions refer to work for 'wet-on-wet') before you apply extra colour or strokes.

HIGHLIGHT

This refers to a lighter colour of the base coat which you apply to an object to make it appear three dimensional. The highlight is always on the opposite side to the shading colour.

SHADE

I use most of these terms as both a verb and a noun so when I tell you to shade the pear it means to apply a colour darker than the base coat of colour. This would be a darker 'shade' of yellow in the case of pears.

FLOATED COLOUR

Wet a flat brush and wipe out the excess water. The brush should be wet but not dripping. Sideload the brush by dipping one corner into the paint, then stroke the brush back and forth on the same spot on the palette until the paint gradually moves across the bristles. Move to the painting and place the edge of the brush with the most paint on, on the outer line to be shaded or highlighted. Paint a shape-following stroke. To reload, rinse the brush thoroughly and repeat the process.

WET-ON-WET TECHNIQUE

This is another form of highlighting and shading that I like to use, especially for larger areas. Touch the brush in Jo Sonja's Retarder before you paint the last layer of base coat, then, before this coat dries, pick up some shading colour in your brush and paint a shape-following stroke, blending the inner edge of stroke into the base coat.

COMMA STROKE

This stroke is just about the most basic and important stroke in all folk painting. It is being able to control the shape of this stroke, that is, getting the fat-to-thin-line of the comma stroke, that opens the doors to so many other painting techniques. The secret for me is in the bounce of the brush and how you control it. Load your round brush with paint of a flowing consistency and touch the point to the painting surface. Press the metal ferrule of the brush (the part that covers the end of the bristles and the wooden handle) towards the surface whilst bringing the handle upright to form a right angle with the surface. This will make the bristles flare and create the 'fat' part of the comma. At the same time as you are creating the shape, start pulling the brush towards you and gradually lifting the bristles off the surface so they return to a point. The 'bounce' is in that pressing down and lifting up to a point so that you can make your stroke as wide or as thin as you require to create the shape. The simplest rule is 'perfection requires practice': the more you paint; the better you get!

PUSH-DAB FLOWERS

These flowers are usually five petalled little numbers that are generally painted with a liner brush or a long round brush. They are made by placing a double-loaded tip of the brush on the piece and pushing the brush away from you slightly, then lifting off abruptly, leaving a tiny circle with both colours in it. Do five of these in a circle, keeping the colours facing the same direction each time.

BOUNCE

This means to tap the brush lightly onto the surface of the painting, with the handle as close to vertical as possible.

DRY BRUSH

This is a technique which is used to apply small amounts of paint to create fuzzy areas. It is usually used for highlighting and involves wiping most of the paint out of the brush and lightly stroking the area you wish to be coloured with the brush, making soft fuzzy lines.

ROUGH BRUSH

This is a term I use to refer to an area of painting that has a solid centre but the edges are brushed out roughly so they are all hairy and soft. It is often a good way to create a soft dark background on a small area on which to layer flowers or fruit. When you brush out the edges, use a dry brush that has most of the paint wiped out of it.

SPONGING

Using a small sponge, a scrunched up rag or a paper towel crumpled into a ball, dip one corner or small section into one colour, then turn the 'sponge' and dip into another colour and again if you need more colours. Press the sponge onto the palette to get rid of the excess paint, then 'bounce' the sponge onto the surface of the piece to be decorated. As you bounce, move from area to area, turning the sponge this way and that so a variety of colours appear next to one another. You may leave the base coat showing through slightly, or cover it completely.

ANTIQUING

There are two forms of antiquing. One uses water-based products, the other oil-based. I generally use the oil-based method and will give you the steps for that, but if you prefer to work with the water-based products, the Jo Sonja's Tech Data Booklet, available from any Jo Sonja Artist's Colour stockist, has complete instructions for a number of methods that are all satisfactory.

Oil-based — After your painting is completely dry, rub the whole area with a medium of six parts of gum arabic turps to four parts of boiled linseed oil mixed together. This should only be a light coat — just enough to seal the area, not dripping from the edges. Then put a touch of Burnt Umber Artist's Oil Paint on a rag and rub it onto the areas of your work that need to be shadowed. If you like the painting to be really dark, then rub the entire piece with oil paint, then rub it off only in the highlight areas. If you decide there are areas of oil paint you need to remove completely, then put some more medium on your rag and rub the Burnt Umber off. Give this layer a few days to dry — the time will vary with the temperature and the humidity — and then proceed with the varnishing.

FINISHING

When the painting is completely dry and has had a few days to cure, varnish with several coats of Jo Sonja Polyurethane Water-based Varnish. Another good trick that will waterproof your piece is a couple of coats of car wax rubbed into the varnish with very fine steel wool, then buffed with a soft cloth. If the painting is to be actually out in the sun and rain, you can renew the wax finish every few months to keep it in good order.

KEY TO PAINTED SAMPLERS

Page 1

1 Simple floated roses (see Wind Chimes)

2 Foxgloves and Canterbury bells (see Watering Can)

3 Climbing roses (see Watering Can)
   and buttercups (see Gardening Apron)

4 Ribbon (see Umbrella Stand)

5 Morning glory (see Bird Feeder)

Page 2

6 Gum tree (see Gumboot Rack)

7 Field poppy (see Gardening Apron)

8 Paper daisy (see Gardening Apron)

9 Pansies (see middle wreath of Gardening Apron)

10 Autumn leaves (see Tablecloth and Directors' Chair)

11 Grapes (see Tablecloth and Director's Chair)

Page 3

12 Old fashioned rose (see Wheelbarrow)

13 Wild roses (see Wheelbarrow)

14 Blueberries (see Wheelbarrow)

15 Wheat (see Wheelbarrow)

16 Hollyhocks (see Church Bird House)

17 Lavender (see Church Bird House and Watering Can)

18 Primitive roses (see Umbrella Stand)

THE WATERING CAN

ABOUT THIS PIECE

I have chosen an already painted watering can because I have had so much difficulty in the past with treating metal surfaces. I usually have the old metal sandblasted and then spray coated, which has worked out well, but any new metal that I have used (and plenty of you will have been able to buy the new galvanised metal buckets and things that are now available for folk artists) has given me a lot of trouble when trying to get the base coat to stay on.

I have ended up having most of my pieces professionally sprayed and have had the most success with automobile undercoat or primer. I must stress, though, that different people have different success with other means, so I think it is a case of everyone finding what works best for themselves. I was very pleased, however, to have success with this pre-base-coated watering can because, when I bought it, it was treated with a surface that I believed could not be painted on, that is, gloss enamelled paint. Fortunately, after I sanded it with the finest sandpaper I had, which is virtually a burnishing paper, it flattened the surface well enough for the folk art paint to cling very nicely.

The watering can also has the advantage of being totally functional because it was sold as a ready-to-use watering can, which means it doesn't have to be put up on the shelf to be admired, it can actually be a practical piece.

PALETTE

Warm White	Red Earth	Yellow Oxide
Raw Sienna	Yellow Light	Turner's Yellow
Titanium White	Norwegian Orange	Burgundy
Napthol Red Light	Teal Green	Green Oxide
Jade	Brown Earth	Plum Pink
Sapphire	Ultramarine	French Blue
Black		

EXTRA MATERIALS NEEDED

sea sponge	magic tape	old stubby brush

PREPARATION

If you are dealing with gloss painted metal, as I have mentioned before, you will need to sand very lightly using the finest sandpaper you can buy, otherwise you

Scale line equals 100 mm

To enlarge to size used in project, simply use an
enlarging photocopier and enlarge line to 100 mm.

Watering Can

will put scratches in the surface of the paint which could show up through the decorative painting. When the surface is ready, you place the magic tape diagonally across the top half of the watering can in parallel lines. It is not necessary to be very accurate about the placing of the tape, as I feel that if it is put on with careful measuring and precision it loses some of the spontaneous look that seems to go with these cottage garden patterns. Place the tape going all one way first, so that you have a series of parallel strips of tape.

Load a large round No. 4 brush with Warm White and paint the strips of watering can that show between the tape, using as many coats as is necessary to cover the background colour of the watering can completely. Allow to dry. I use the same strips of tape to repeat the process on the opposite diagonal, placing the tape across the painted stripes already there and using the same distances between the strips of tape. Then paint another series of white stripes between the magic tape until you have used enough coats to cover both the previous stripes and the background colour of the watering can. I only painted the lattice on the top half of the watering can because the paint becomes fairly thick and if you continued the lattice work down onto the bottom half of the watering can the actual extra dimensions of the paint might show through the garden at the bottom.

Using a dampened sea sponge dipped in Teal Green, Green Oxide and Jade (that is a little on each section of the sponge), bounce the sponge all over the bottom half of the watering can, turning it all the time so that you get a variety of greens working their way up the watering can. I always try to keep the Teal Green heaviest at the bottom and the Green Oxide and Teal towards the middle and the Jade at the top of the sponged area. I bring the sponging right up the watering can until I cover the bottom of the lattice and then bring a little bit here and there up the sides, as you can see from the photograph. Allow this to dry.

PROCEDURE

I find my students have the most success with the cottage garden patterns when not using a traced pattern, but I have included the different layers of flowers on the green step-by-step colour pages towards the front of the book, so, if you are in doubt about how to paint the flowers onto the piece, please check there. If you need a pattern, I would recommend that you trace each type of flower separately in rows and then apply them to the piece as you reach the spot where they are required.

1. **Roses** — Using a liner brush and a light brown mix gained by mixing Brown Earth and Raw Sienna, detail in the stems of the climbing roses up and across the back of the lattice. Try to make these twine in and out of the lattice, with some stems going over the front and other stems coming in from behind. Mix a touch of Black with Yellow Light to make an olive green and, still using the liner brush, paint in the rose leaves with tiny comma strokes.

   The pink climbing roses are made from a mix of Red Earth, Yellow Oxide and a lot of White, giving a soft apricot. The first step is to base coat the circles and ovals of the roses. While the apricot roses are drying, base in the yellow roses on the other side in a mix of Yellow Oxide and White to make a creamy yellow. These will probably need two coats to get a good coverage over the background colours. Then sideload a No. 6 flat brush with a darker apricot mix, that is, the rose base coat plus more Red Earth, and float a C-stroke at the base of each of the circles and ovals. At the top of each of the circles and ovals, make the throat by floating a tiny C-stroke facing the same direction as the base shading. The yellow roses are floated in the same way, with Yellow Oxide for the base and Raw Sienna for the throats.

   The bush roses are painted similarly, except that the white rose on the left is a mix of Warm White with a touch of Raw Sienna and the red rose is a bright tomato red made by mixing Napthol Red Light and Red Earth. To make a soft shading colour for the white rose, I mixed a touch of the pink and a touch of the Raw Sienna in with the white base colour to get a warm beige, and shaded the white rose and its throat with this colour. The red rose shading is Burgundy mixed with a touch of Brown Earth. I find that the Burgundy over the straight tomato red is a little too transparent, but if you add a little Brown Earth or one of the darker colours, it becomes a good shading colour. The trunks and stems of the bush roses are the same colour as the stems of the climbing roses. The leaves are a fraction darker than the climbing roses, with a little more Black in the mix, so that they stand out from the background sponging.

2. **Canterbury Bells** — Using a liner brush and Teal Green, paint in the stem of the Canterbury bells, extending about two-thirds of the way down the side of the watering can. Change to a No. 2 or 3 round brush and mix a soft blue from Sapphire Blue, White and a touch of French Blue and paint rounded triangles of the bells up and down the stems around the watering can.

When these are dry, sideload a flat No. 6 brush with Ultramarine and float a shading at the base of each of the bells. Change back to a liner brush and, with a little bit of Plum Pink mixed into the Ultramarine to make a soft purple, draw a wriggly line around the edge of each bell. If you check with the step-by-step colour pages you will see this clearly.

3. **Queen Anne's Lace** — Load the liner brush with Jade, remembering to water it down so that it flows in thin lines, and paint in the stems of all the Queen Anne's lace. At the top of each main stalk is a little umbrella of stems, each coming back to a central point. Next load an old stubby brush with Titanium White. Dab some of the paint out of it on practice paper, then bounce some fluffy curves and circles on the ends of the umbrella stems of the Queen Anne's lace.

4. **Foxgloves** — These flowers are in various mixes of Plum Pink and White, or Yellow Oxide and White. They are just about on the same level as the Queen Anne's lace, although some of them are staggered.

Start by using a No. 3 round brush and a thin mix of either Yellow Oxide or Plum Pink and base in the triangular shape of each of the foxgloves, depending on how you want the colour shown. For the paler pink foxgloves, mix some White with the Plum Pink for a paler pink background. This will be semi-transparent and you will see the green showing through some of them. Next mix more White with the base colour to make a solid colour and, using a No. 3 round brush again, paint in little dabs of solid colour to represent each of the blossoms in the foxgloves.

I was asked if I was sure there was such a thing as a yellow foxglove and I can say, 'Yes, there is', as I had one and it died. Next year I am going to try for the pink, maybe they will be hardier.

When the blossoms are all dry, sideload a flat No. 6 or smaller brush with the straight Yellow Oxide or Plum Pink and float in a tiny C-stroke at the bottom of each of the teardrop-shaped blossoms. Paint in the stems from the bottom row of blossoms, if you feel you need them. I brought my lavender bushes up high enough in front of the foxgloves so I didn't need to bother with stems.

5. **Lavender bushes** — Mix a pale green using Jade and perhaps a little more White and a touch of Black (this will give a pale grey-green). Paint in upside down 'umbrella spines' of stems somewhat below the foxgloves, but reaching up almost to them. The stems need to be fairly dense, in keeping with the bushy nature of this garden, but as they become thinner at the top you should be able to see a bit of the background showing through.

   Mix a few shades of lavender from Plum Pink and Ultramarine or Burgundy and Ultramarine. I try to put a variety of shades of lavender on each bush to give the impression of three dimensions. Using the liner brush, load with these mixes of lavender and bounce small sideways half-commas up each of the stalks, painted in soft green. The dabs start large and diminish as they go up the stalks. If the lavenders are a little too dark, as they probably will be if you use the straight pinks and blues, add a little white to the mix at various times so that you get some lighter mauves.

6. **Daisies** — Using a liner brush and a yellow-green mix made by combining Green Oxide, Turner's Yellow and White, stroke in some very random spiky-looking stems below the lavender.

   Change to a No. 3 round brush and paint the daisy petals, using short half-comma strokes, with the colour Titanium White. Paint the centres in Red Earth with a touch of Brown Earth at the base. You can do this either with a line of Brown Earth at the base of the red centre or by double-loading the No. 3 brush and dabbing in the centres so that the Brown Earth appears at the base of each one.

7. **Daffodils** — Using Turner's Yellow and a No. 3 round brush, paint short fat comma strokes in a five-stroke star pattern. Mix some Norwegian Orange with the Turner's Yellow to make a light orange and base in a circle of light orange in the centre of the star pattern.

   When this is dry, change to the liner brush and straight Norwegian Orange and paint a wriggly line around the light orange circle. The stems for the daffodils are a light yellowy green. If you have a gap to fill in, put some leaves coming off the stems of the daffodils as well.

8. **Forget-Me-Nots** — With a liner brush double-loaded in Ultramarine and White, place 'push-dab' clusters of little flowers all around the base of the watering can. Refer to the description of these flowers in Terms and Techniques of Folk Art, as well as checking in the step-by-step colour pages. I use these flowers to fill in as much of the base of the watering can as necessary.

FINISHING

When the painting is completely dry and has had a few days to cure, varnish with several coats of Jo Sonja Polyurethane Water-based Varnish. To waterproof your piece two or three coats of car wax rubbed into the varnish with very fine steel wool, then buffed with a soft cloth will create a weatherproof surface. If the painting is to be actually out in the sun and rain, you can renew the wax finish every few months to keep it in good order.

UMBRELLA STAND

ABOUT THIS PIECE

The landscapes that are featured in this book are based on my experiences of having lived in the New South Wales' Riverina, and much travelling down through Eastern Australia. I have always loved the area known as the Gundagai Hills and, even though the painted landscape is primitive in its lack of detail, it reminds me of the view to the left and right of the highway in this area. I originally developed a pattern for a towel rail based on an American primitive landscape, but things progessed from there and I found the application to the Australian landscape so exciting with our red iron oxide soils and our green and gold hills. I have taken artistic licence quite a few times in the landscapes, such as putting freshly shorn sheep miles away from the shearing shed and using corrugated iron vanes on the windmills, not to mention growing vegetables and pumpkins in what appears to be perfectly good sheep country! Hopefully, people will forgive me, given the overall effect.

PALETTE

Sapphire	Warm White	Nimbus Grey
Green Oxide	Jade	Black
Raw Sienna	Turner's Yellow	Yellow Oxide
Red Earth	Gold Oxide	Brown Earth
Teal Green	Rich Gold	Napthol Red Light

PREPARATION

As this is an old milk can I had it sandblasted and primed professionally, but when putting a landscape pattern on something other than a piece of metalware I usually just base coat in cream or white. When this is dry, apply only the hill line that touches the sky. This line will be painted over here and there, but it gives you an idea of how much sky you intend to have and how much land. I generally find that two-thirds sky and one-third land, or a little more than one-third, is generally acceptable to the eye.

PROCEDURE

1. **Sky** — To create the blended look of the blue sky fading to a lighter colour on the horizon line, I use nothing less than a 1 inch (25 mm) flat brush. If the piece is larger than average, as the milk can was, I use a 2″ (50 mm) flat brush. Load one corner of a wet brush into straight Sapphire, or if that is a little

too vibrant for you, a mix of Sapphire and White, and then load the other corner of the brush in White. Blend these colours out a little on the palette and then, using long strokes and starting at the darkest point, which is the top of the sky, or the top of your piece, blend the blue and white down towards the horizon, always keeping the white-loaded corner of the brush towards the horizon and the blue-loaded corner towards the top of the piece.

The most important thing about this type of blending, I find, is to be able to do long, continuous strokes. Go right from one side of the piece to the other, if you can. With the milk can, I found it a little bit more difficult, but even then I tried to do a stroke that would take in at least a third of the can before I moved back in the other direction. Another important thing to remember is to keep the strokes horizontal when you get down to the hill line. Don't try to follow the contours of the hills. If necessary, you can put the pattern back over the sky, but it is important that all the strokes be blended into each other, without any noticeable curves. Continue to load the brush with blue on one side and white on the other and blend with the long horizontal strokes on the piece. The final effect you require is a very bright blue at the top, fading down very gradually to a much lighter blue on the horizon.

actual size

2. **Clouds** — The clouds are painted by loading a No. 3 round brush with White and painting a curved comma stroke across each of the fluffy tops of the clouds. Put the brush down and put your finger into the wet paint and pull it down while tapping gently on the blue background until the paint dries on your finger. This will give you a thick white curve at the top of the fluffy cloud, blending down to a stippled effect on the lower section of the cloud. When you have painted and stippled in enough of the curves in the cloud, holding a No. 3 round brush up on the tip, put in a few light, dry-brushed straight strokes across the bottom of the cloud with the same White. Obviously this only applies to those floating in the sky, not the clouds floating on the horizon.

3. **Hills** — Using a round brush (the size of which will be dictated by the size of the piece you are painting), paint in the hills, starting from the back, or the horizon line, and working forwards. The colours that you use will be entirely up to you. I always recommend that the paler green, such as the Jade, goes on the back horizon of the hills with perhaps one mid-green, that is, the Green Oxide, to space them out. Then, as you come forward in the picture, bring in the Red Earth and the Gold Oxide hills, interspersed with some darker and some middle green. You can see from the photograph in the colour pages how it is done. The middle hills I usually reserve for the Red Earth and the Gold Oxide and a medium brown that is a mix of Brown Earth and Gold Oxide. These are meant to represent the ploughed or the planted areas. Obviously the important thing is to have no two hills of the same colour joining each other.

The roads I try to make a lighter colour, usually a Raw Sienna and White mix.

The lakes or dams that I have included in the pattern can be painted in a pale blue mix of Sapphire and White. I do this advisedly, the implication being that the blue sky is reflecting in the water. This saves painting them another shade of brown, which would just confuse things with the hills. When all the hills are filled in with colour in their varying shades of greens and browns, shade them on their upper surface with a float of the next darker green or brown. So the Jade hills are shaded with Green Oxide, the Green Oxide with Teal Green, the Teal Green hills with Teal

Green mixed with a little Black, and then in the browns, the medium brown hills are shaded with Brown Earth, the Red Earth hills are also shaded with Brown Earth and the Gold Oxide hills are shaded with Red Earth and so on. Sometimes it helps to shade the valleys with a float of darker colour as well, but you have to be careful here not to have each hill looking like a padded quilted area, which it can easily do if you encase it with the floated colour.

4. **The Foliage** — With the foliage I generally refer to all the trees and shrubs that are growing between the hills, on top of the hills and beside the houses, as opposed to the crops which are just running over the hills. Using a No. 3 round brush loaded with Green Oxide, double-load with Teal Green and tip the brush in Raw Sienna on one occasion and Jade on others. Using short dabbing strokes, fill in all the foliage you see on the pattern, making sure there is a variety of greens in each area. If there is an obvious row of trees, I try to keep the Jade or the Raw Sienna on the same side as each of the trees. If the shrubs back into a hill line, then I try to keep the Teal Green towards the base of the shrub area at ground level. The most important thing is to keep the strokes short and dabby so that the contour of the shrubs is random and rough.

5. **The Buildings** — The homesteads or cottages are always painted Warm White with the roofs a mix of Napthol Red Light and Red Earth. I tend to paint all the hills in as though the buildings don't exist and then place the pattern on for the buildings and paint them over the top of the hills. The shearing sheds and the windmills are painted with Nimbus Grey to which a little White has been added. Then to draw in the corrugated lines and outline the sheds, I use straight Nimbus Grey. The windows, as you can see, are Black with Nimbus Grey detailed work over the top. The shearing shed doors are medium brown. The fence posts are the lighter Nimbus Grey mix with a detailing using the liner brush in Black. The fence wires are also Nimbus Grey.

6. **The Animals** — The sheep in the pattern are Suffolks, simply because they stand out better with their black noses and legs. I am not averse to Merinos or any other breed of sheep being included. The ones that are in the distance are painted using a liner brush loaded with Warm White and dabby strokes to create

little fluffy caterpillar shapes, each with a dot black nose and four black legs poking out from underneath, except for the ones sitting down, of course.

The ducks on the lakes or dams are done with a liner brush and Warm White and with a tiny yellow beak dotted in the front of each of them. There can be ducks or chickens on the edge of the lakes.

7. **Crops** — Choose some of the Red Earth and Gold Oxide hills to become ploughed areas. I usually indicate these with wavy darker lines, using either Brown Earth on the Red Earth hills or Red Earth on the Gold Oxide. With the other crops it is really a case of botanical licence again. You have to choose what sort of plants and what rows they will be in. The only important aspect is that the rows of plants or grasses follow the contours of the hills, as you can see in the picture.

8. **Primitive Rose Swag** (on the shoulder of the milk can) — First of all, trace the outline of the leaves that are showing behind the roses and transfer this to the piece. With a large round or flat brush, base coat this in Teal Green. Double-load the brush filled with Teal and Jade and paint the sides and centres of the main leaves with double fat comma strokes. Trace the roses in the patterns just as ovals or circles and transfer them onto the green leaf background when it is dry. Mix a little White and Red Earth for an apricot pink, and base coat the circles and ovals of the roses until the background is entirely covered. Then with a flat brush sideloaded in Red Earth, float two C-strokes of colour, one around the base of the circle or the oval, and a tiny one above the first stroke for the throat. These will not all be pointing in the same direction, so the top and the base shading will need to make the roses point out from the centre of the swag.

Mix a lighter pink, with more White added to the base colour, and, using a No. 3 brush, paint a series of curved comma strokes around one side of the circle or oval of the roses in this paler pink. (Try to keep the light comma strokes on the same side of each of the roses, but obviously if the rose throats are all pointing in different directions this will be hard. You just have to make an arbitrary decision on where you are going to put the light side of each rose.) Make sure you start each curved comma stroke a little outside the circle or oval, or they will look like strange little beehives instead of roses. Repeat this process with the round brush loaded with Red Earth and paint curved comma strokes on the opposite side of the circle or oval of the roses. Bring the tails of the comma strokes over the top of the paler ones' tails and then, with a lighter pink in your brush, dry brush a few zigzags over the area where the curved comma strokes overlap. Place one light comma stroke at the back of each throat of the roses. Paint some light pink dots in the centre of each of the roses. Finally, load the liner brush with Titanium White and paint a number of small white flowers with yellow centres, according to the pattern. These are small white flowers with mini comma strokes for their petals. Some of them are only half flowers poking out from behind the roses.

9. **The Ribbon** — Load a No. 3 round brush with a pale blue made by mixing Sapphire Blue and White, and sideload in Rich Gold. Paint in the ribbon loops and tails, using a thin-fat-thin stroke. This is made by starting on the point of the brush, pressing down to flare the bristles, then lifting up on to the point again with unequal sequence, following the pattern as near as possible.

FINISHING

When the painting is completely dry and has had a few days to cure, varnish with several coats of Jo Sonja Polyurethane Water-based Varnish. To waterproof your piece, two or three coats of car wax rubbed into the varnish with very fine steel wool, then buffed with a soft cloth, will create a weatherproof surface. If the painting is to be actually out in the sun and rain, you can renew the wax finish every few months to keep it in good order.

Scale line equals 100 mm

To enlarge to size used in project, simply use an enlarging photocopier and enlarge line to 100 mm.

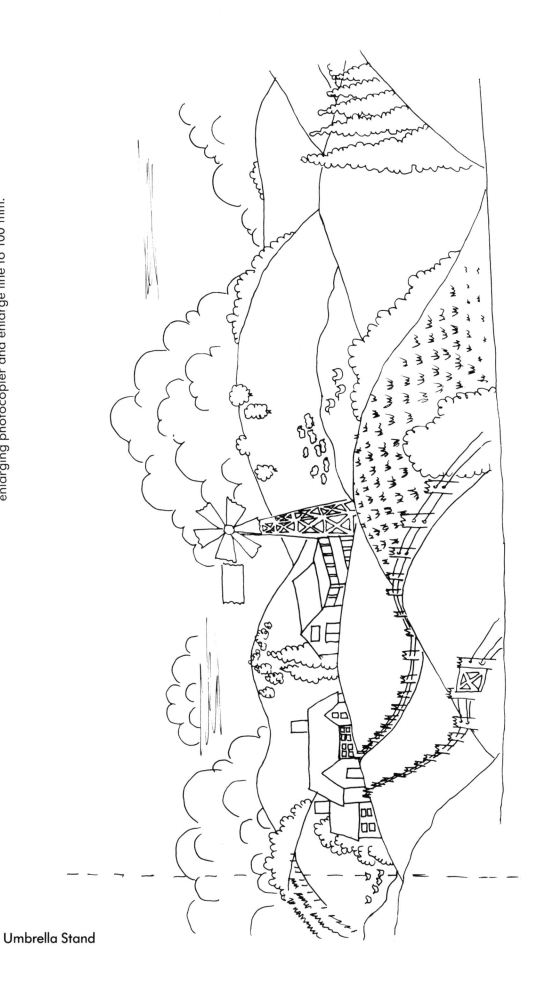

Scale line equals 100 mm

To enlarge to size used in project, simply use an enlarging photocopier and enlarge line to 100 mm.

Umbrella Stand

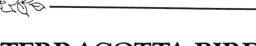

TERRACOTTA BIRD FEEDER

ABOUT THIS PIECE

Because we have a few fairly large parrots in our garden I decided that if I was going to paint a bird feeder, it should be able to stand a bit of weight and be able to accommodate many birds at one time. It also needed to be the type that if it fell down it would damage the cat that was sitting underneath waiting for the birds to fall in its mouth! There are plenty of other styles of bird feeders, and obviously painting on the wooden ones is very successful, but I thought a terracotta bird feeder was a little different.

PALETTE

Sapphire
Black
Green Oxide

French Blue
Titanium White
Jade

Teal Green
Turner's Yellow

PREPARATION

As with all terracotta, I sealed this piece first with Jo Sonja All Purpose Sealer, inside and out. You could, in fact, base coat the piece all over in the background mix of Teal Green with a touch of Black, but I am rather fond of the terracotta colour in the garden so this time I chose only to base coat under the area where the flowers are.

Roughly brush the black-green colour under the flower area, according to the pattern, and then, using a round brush, go around the edges of the dry-brushed area and paint in a number of small leaves so the points poke out from the black-green area in this same colour. Trace and apply the pattern as nearly as possible so that it fits around the two sides of the bird feeder. Because this is a curved surface, there is a gap in the pattern which you have to overlap, but I think it is just a case of transferring one of the other flowers, or a few extra leaves, anywhere that you feel there is a sad space.

PROCEDURE

1. **Leaves** — Using a No. 3 round brush, base coat all the larger leaves that you can see in Green Oxide and add a few more if you feel the spaces of black-

green are too large. Paint the leaves entirely, not going around the blossoms in the pattern, because it is better to come back over the top with the blossoms and then we will repaint the leaves that are superimposed on the blossoms at a later date. When the large Green Oxide leaves are dry, with a flat brush, float some straight Teal Green down the centre of each leaf for a centre vein and around the larger back end of the leaves.

2. **Blossoms** — Transfer the blossom pattern over the top of the Green Oxide leaves. Base coat the trumpet flowers with their open sections in White and their trumpet sections behind the white petals in a pale blue, which is made by mixing Sapphire and White and a touch of French Blue to make a very soft pale blue. Obviously, over such a dark background, these will probably take several coats.

Load a medium-sized flat brush with French Blue and put a float of this colour at the ends of all the pale blue trumpets and underneath the white turned-over edges of the petals. There should be a float of French Blue wherever the white ends of the flowers are superimposed over the pale blue trumpets.

Then float the centres of each of the trumpet flowers, again with French Blue, trying to make the edges of the float as blended as possible. If you do end up with some stark edges, once you have completed the stroke, go back in with the clean corner of the brush and softly blend out these strong areas.

Load the flat brush in the first pale blue mix and float this blue around the outer edge of all the white petals. This blue must be very pale and must blend nicely over the white or it will look a little strange.

Finally, to complete the blossoms, use a liner brush loaded with Turner's Yellow to paint in very fine filaments poking out of the darkened centres of each blossom. These can have a few dots on the ends of each of them as well.

3. **Stems** — Load a liner brush with thinned Jade Green and paint in all the tendrils and sepals and stems attached to the blossoms. Use some of the Jade to create centre veins in the smaller leaves on the edges of the pattern. Finally, go back to the Green Oxide leaves where some of them are overlapping the blossoms in the pattern, and paint them over the top of the white blossoms again.

FINISHING

When the painting is completely dry and has had a few days to cure, varnish with several coats of Jo Sonja Polyurethane Water-based Varnish. The terracotta will also work with the car wax rubbed into the varnish with very fine steel wool, then buffed with a soft cloth. If the painting is to be actually out in the sun and rain, you can renew the wax finish every few months to keep it in good order.

Bird Feeder

Scale line equals 100 mm

To enlarge to size used in project, simply use an enlarging photocopier and enlarge line to 100 mm.

CHURCH BIRD HOUSE

ABOUT THIS PIECE

A friend of mine makes these churches in various sizes. There is not much pattern to put on them and most of it is very simple painting, but they look very attractive in a rambling cottage garden.

PALETTE

Red Earth	Gold Oxide	Yellow Oxide
Turner's Yellow	Plum Pink	Storm Blue
Nimbus Grey	Warm White	Raw Sienna
Teal Green	Green Oxide	Jade

PREPARATION

The walls, front and back of the church are base coated in Warm White with a little Raw Sienna to make a warm cream colour. The roof is a silvery grey, made by mixing Nimbus Grey with Warm White. The trim is Black. The churches are usually made of hard wood and so need quite a bit of sanding back to get a smooth finish. Once the base coated walls and roof are dry, add the black detailing on the gutters and the bird stand and the extra bits on the bird house. Apply the pattern lightly to the roof, for the shingles, and to the windows. Next take a damp sponge and dip it in a small amount of Teal Green, Green Oxide and Jade and sponge around the base of the two side walls and the back walls, bouncing and turning the sponge so you get an uneven coloured foliage effect. Include the base in this green sponging, because it is all part of the garden that is around the church. Do not sponge the green up over the windows, only below and between them. The green sponging should go about a quarter of the way up the walls, maybe a little more in some places, but certainly not much further than a third of the way up beside the windows. In order to lighten the green sponging a little, when I had finished with the Teal Green, Green

Oxide and Jade mix, and while it was still wet I picked up a little bit of Turner's Yellow and Yellow Oxide and lightly sponged over the top of the green here and there so that the yellow blended into it and made it less of a bottle green and more of a light springtime green. When the sponging is dry, apply the pattern for the flowers and the ivy around the base of the church.

PROCEDURE

1. **Roof** — Draw up the roof with a pencil and a ruler into approximately 2″ (5 cm) squares, each row of squares staggered with the one above. This is to represent shingles or slate tiles on the roof, which must overlap unevenly. Draw the tiles in over the pencil lines with a black technical pen or a fine-tipped waterproof felt pen, curving each of the lower corners. Then load a flat brush (a reasonably large one, such as a No. 8) in straight Nimbus Grey, blend into the brush and then float along the underside of each of the tiles.

2. **Windows** — I used two reds and two yellows in the windows. The main thing is to keep the diamond shapes with the same colour from butting up against each other. Start off with Red Earth and paint random diamonds, with most of them being at the base of the window and petering out to one or two in each row by about two-thirds up the window. Next, load up the brush with Gold Oxide and base in more of the lower diamonds in the windows, then fill in some more with Yellow Oxide, and finally finish off the rest with Turner's Yellow. As you can see from the picture the effect is that the darker colours are at the base of the window, fading to the lighter Turner's Yellow at the top. It is very much a random pattern and whatever arrangement of colours you choose will be the right one.

3. **Hollyhocks** — With a liner brush loaded in Teal Green, draw in a long wavy stem for each of the hollyhocks on the sides and back of the church. Change to a No. 3 round brush loaded in a light pink made by mixing Plum Pink with White, and paint in an amoeba-shaped circle up and down the stems of the hollyhocks. With a liner brush loaded first in Teal Green, flick some small caps on the backs of the hollyhocks that are hanging down. Also insert

some green leaves coming off the stem between the blossoms. Change to a lighter mix of Plum Pink and White and outline each blossom, then put a few dots in the centre.

4. **Lavender** — Mix a little Green Oxide with Nimbus Grey to create a soft grey green and, using the liner brush, stroke in an upside-down umbrella shape of stems where each of the lavender bushes are shown. The stems should be quite dense at the bottom and further apart at the top. Mix some Plum Pink and Storm Blue and a little White to create various shades of mauve. With the liner brush, dab in the lavender flowers on the ends of each of the stalks. These flowers start with short sideways dabs that get smaller and smaller as you go up to the top of the stem. It helps to vary the colour a little, having some dark and some blended lavender stalks.

5. **Ivy** — The ivy is painted with a liner brush loaded with Teal Green. Paint the stems of the ivy on the back of the church around the window, then with either a No. 3 round or a heavily loaded liner brush, dab in the little leaves. They are dab strokes with not much shape to them except that they are larger at the main stem and diminish towards the ends of the stems.

6. **Front** — The half-round dowels around the bird house opening are painted in Red Earth and the dowel for the birds to sit on is painted Black. I also painted the inside edge of the front hole Black.

FINISHING

When the painting is completely dry and has had a few days to cure, varnish with several coats of Jo Sonja Polyurethane Water-based Varnish. The car wax finish (see Finishing in 'Terms and Techniques of Folk Art') will work on wood as well, providing there are enough coats of varnish applied first.

Scale line equals 100 mm

To enlarge to size used in project, simply use an
enlarging photocopier and enlarge line to 100 mm.

end of bird house

Scale line equals 100 mm

To enlarge to size used in project, simply use an enlarging photocopier and enlarge line to 100 mm.

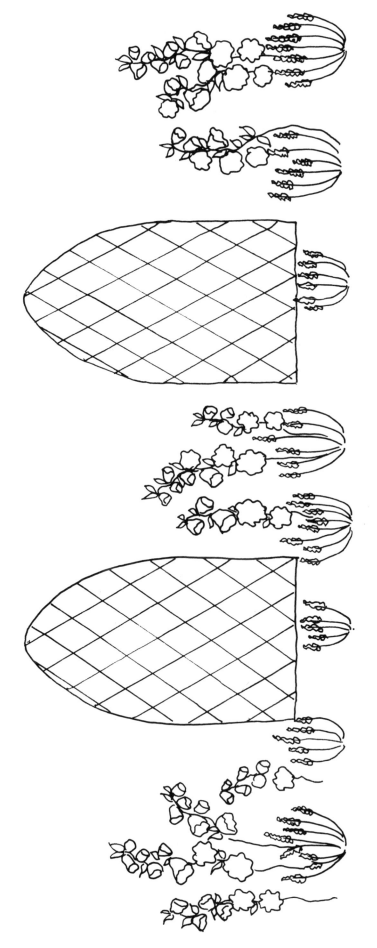

side of bird house

Church Bird House

WHEELBARROW

ABOUT THIS PIECE

I spent an extremely long time searching for a wheelbarrow to paint for this book because I felt no folk-art-in-the-garden book would be complete without one. I saw many modern wheelbarrows made out of wood of various kinds, but the price always gave me a nervous breakdown, so I never followed them up. This wheelbarrow belonged to a neighbour of mine, who kindly donated it for the book. As it is a fairly old-fashioned one, I thought it was an ideal shape to paint. I have only included a pattern for the side, but it might be one of those on-going pieces that gets added to over time. My next problem with the wheelbarrow was that I wanted to paint it with the pumpkins in it because it looked so colourful. If I chose a completely floral pattern, I felt it wouldn't be entirely appropriate, because wheelbarrows are meant to be useful items that carry a lot of things other than flowers. So, in order to make the pattern a little more rustic, I have included wilder-looking poppies, blueberries and wheat as well as the cabbage roses. The pattern has been antiqued, but it does not necessarily need it, as the flowers, with the berries and the grain, work quite well on the chocolate brown background without antiquing.

PALETTE

Titanium White	Warm White	Red Earth
Brown Earth	Napthol Red Light	Burgundy
Yellow Light	Black	Yellow Oxide
Turner's Yellow	Sapphire	French Blue
Green Oxide	Jade	Raw Sienna
Gold Oxide		

PREPARATION

The wheelbarrow was fairly clean when I acquired it, but I still steel brushed it, rinsed it out with vinegar and water and dried it thoroughly with a hair dryer. It was then base coated with a spray rust-proofing paint that can be bought in many colours. The paint was advertised as a semi-gloss, but I found after three coats it had only a mild gloss on it and when I sanded it very, very lightly where I wanted to put the painting, it didn't destroy the base coat. Before painting on the flowers, mix up a teddy bear brown colour from Gold Oxide and Brown Earth. Paint an oval on the side of the wheelbarrow the size you wish to go under the flower spray. When that is completely dry, using a No. 3 or 4 round brush, paint a series of curved comma strokes all the way around the edge of the oval in straight Gold Oxide.

PROCEDURE

1. **Background Leaves** — For these leaves I used an olive green made by adding a touch of Black to Yellow Light, and then painted in the larger leaves in such a way that I did all the shading and the stroke work of the veins before going on to any other leaves. Shade the leaves by sideloading the olive green with Black. If you are not fond of the warmer colours which the olive green tends to start you on, by all means use a Teal Green and Raw Sienna or some other dark green that suits you. These large leaves are mainly background to the other flowers but it is important that they are dark enough to throw the lighter-coloured flowers out to the front of the pattern.

2. **Roses** — This style of rose is based on the cabbage rose in my garden called the Prioress. I really like the cabbage roses without too much of a frill and a very round bowl. On the step-by-step colour pages I simplified the design slightly and chose a red rose to demonstrate. The important thing with these roses is to stick to the pattern.

   I shall speak of the red, yellow and white roses collectively and describe the procedure in terms of dark, medium and light. When you first apply the pattern of the roses, don't put in the petal outlines, only put in the outer circumference of each rose. For each coloured rose you will need three values — a medium, light and dark. I would mix these in advance and keep them on a wet palette. For the red roses, the light value is Napthol Red Light plus Vermillion, the medium value is Napthol Red Light plus Red Earth and the dark value is Brown Earth mixed with a small amount of the medium value. For the yellow rose, the light value is Yellow Light, the medium value is Turner's Yellow and the dark value is Yellow Oxide mixed with a little Raw Sienna. For the white rose, the light value is Titanium White, the medium value is Warm White with a touch of Raw Sienna and the dark value is the same medium value with Raw Sienna and a touch of Brown Earth.

Take your medium value mix for each rose and, with a round brush, base in the circle and the frill petals all in the one colour until it is completely opaque with no transparent lines. Then bring your pattern back and place the petal lines on top of this dry base coated area. Normally I am very relaxed about structure and pattern and tell my students to make it the way they would like it to look. In this case, however, I have to stress that the way the pattern is put on is crucial to the success of the finished rose. The curve of each of the petals has to be pointing in the right direction to give the appearance of roundness to the rose. So when you place the pattern back on the base coated area make sure that it is as accurate as possible and easily readable when you remove the pattern. Once you have based in the middle value and have the pattern of the petals on the base coated rose, load a flat brush in the darkest value of the colour (for example, with the yellow rose this will be Raw Sienna and Yellow Oxide mix, with the red rose it will be the Brown Earth mix and with the white rose it will be a little Raw Sienna mixed with a little Brown Earth and White to create a dark beige). Float two semi-circles on the medium value area, one at the top of the circle for the throat and the other at the base of the central circle, just inside the outer petal line. When this is dry, double-load the flat brush in the medium value of the rose plus the highlight value on one side and, following the petal lines, C-stroke in the petals, working from the throat down to the bottom of the bowl. I find it necessary to double-load the flat brush with both the base colour and the highlight colour because if you float these petals they don't look substantial enough. In doing this you might lose a little of your lower bowl floated stroke but you can replace that once the petal lines are dry. Then change to the smaller flat brush and double-load it again with the medium value and the highlight value and stroke around the outer rim of the frill petals. At the back of the throat, place a few of the highlight-loaded petals in a scalloped shape. I sometimes do this with a round brush rather than a flat. Please do this if you are more comfortable shading with a round instead of a flat.

3. **Wheat** — Using a liner brush loaded with Yellow Oxide tipped with White, paint in the stems of the wheat heads. Make sure you take the stem right to the end of the head. Don't stop at the bottom of the wheat seeds. Change to a No. 2 round brush, load with Yellow Oxide tipped with White and paint in the wheat leaves. Then load the tip of the same brush with Yellow Oxide and a tiny bit of White and dab the wheat heads in on the end of the stems with small teardrop strokes, starting large and getting smaller and smaller as they go to the end of the wheat head. If you have room, or if you wish, you can put a few hairs at the end of each of the wheat stalks.

4. **Smaller Leaves** — The small leaves or foliage that come out from the centre of the pattern are done in a variety of greens, mainly a medium value with a light value green, and are stroked in with small shape-following strokes. With a double-loaded No. 3 round brush, paint pointed comma strokes that are taken back in under the flowers. That is, start at the point of the stroke and then gently press down with the brush and pull it into the centre of the design.

   At this time you could also do the stems and the small leaves for the blueberries.

5. **Blueberries** — The blueberries are based in with a mix of Sapphire and a little White. Sideload the round brush with French Blue and put in a shade stroke. When that is dry, sideload with a little lighter Sapphire and White mix and put in the highlight stroke. If you wish to float the highlight and the shading, that's fine, but be careful the two do not overlap and create a messy area. Finally, change to the liner brush and put a tiny C-stroke in Black at the end of each berry. When that is dry, paint three or four fine, spiky hairs coming out of the little black C-stroke at the end of each berry.

6. **Poppies** — These poppies, being salmon coloured, display my willingness to be botanically incorrect, but I am sure that in time there will be a poppy of this colour and then I will be exonerated! Mix Red Earth and White to get a shell pink and, with a No. 3 round brush, base in the poppy petals according to the step-by-step directions in the colour pages. Change to a flat brush and with a slightly darker pink (that is one with more Red Earth in it), float some sharp U-strokes into the base of each of the petals where the centre will be. Change back to the round brush

loaded with the original base colour with a side load of Titanium White and paint a white tip around the edge of each of the petals. Where the petals are turning in rather than sitting out, reverse the side that the White is on your round brush so that the tip of the petal is painted white and not the centre. Finally, with a liner brush loaded in Brown Earth with a touch of Black, dab in a centre into each of the poppies, the ones that can be seen. When this is dry, sideload the liner brush in a little Yellow Oxide or Turner's Yellow and Brown Earth and dab in some small pollen dots around one side of each of the centres.

FINISHING

I antiqued the painted area lightly, once the paint had cured and dried in a few days. I then base coated the entire painted area with Jo Sonja's Polyurethane Varnish, and before I use it outside I will apply coats of wax as described in Finishing, 'Terms and Techniques of Folk Art'.

Scale line equals 100 mm

To enlarge to size used in project, simply use an
enlarging photocopier and enlarge line to 100 mm.

Wheelbarrow

GUMBOOT RACK

ABOUT THIS PIECE

I was discussing gardens, gumboots and wellington boots with a friend one day and we were musing on the possibility of creating some sort of boot rack that would allow the boots to drain and hopefully keep spiders out; the boots would be ready-to-wear at a moment's notice. From that germ of an idea I came up with this slightly whimsical gumboot rack. It is a piece that could be very heavily antiqued and left outside without worrying about whether it became dirty or not. I think it is also a very useful style. It is easy to make, being two pieces of 19 mm (¾") thick pine with three 38 mm (1½") dowels between them. I have attached knobs to the ends of the dowels to make it easier to dismantle and to move, if necessary. But if you wish to fix the dowel in and putty over the end of the hole, then that would be fine, too.

PALETTE

Sapphire	Warm White	Nimbus Grey
Green Oxide	Jade	Black
Raw Sienna	Turner's Yellow	Yellow Oxide
Red Earth	Gold Oxide	Brown Earth
Teal Green	Rich Gold	Napthol Red Light

PREPARATION

Base coat the inside faces of the boots ends with Red Earth and the dowel pieces with either Teal Green or Black (whichever you would prefer). Enlarge the line on the pattern to 100 mm to get the full sized pattern. The painted side of each boot needs to be sealed and sanded with Jo Sonja All Purpose Sealer.

PROCEDURE

Refer to the pattern for the umbrella stand and paint in the sky and clouds according to those directions. Next place the hill pattern onto the piece, but do not put the tree in — leave that until last. Paint all the hills, the houses, the crops, the foliage and everything else before you complete the tree. (Refer to these items in the umbrella stand pattern for instructions.) Once these are dry, trace the tree pattern in over the top of the painting. Base coat the tree trunk and branches in Warm White. When this is dry, sideload the brush in a very little of a pale mix of Nimbus Grey and Warm White and shade each of the stems or branches of the tree. With a liner brush and a mixture of greens, lightly stroke in some grass at the base of the tree so that it looks like it is sitting in a small patch of grass and not on top of the painting. Try to match the grass to the colour of the hill that it is on. The foliage of the tree is a series of dabbed areas, starting with Green Oxide and changing to a mix of Green Oxide and Brown Earth for the shading on the underside of the tree areas. Then highlight these areas with a little Green Oxide sideloaded in Raw Sienna and Yellow Oxide to give the lighter tops of the tree branches. The main thing is to dab randomly and make the edges of the green areas quite fuzzy and dangly.

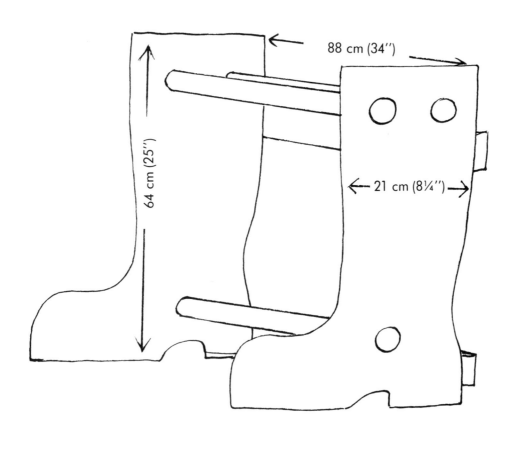

88 cm (34″)

64 cm (25″)

21 cm (8¼″)

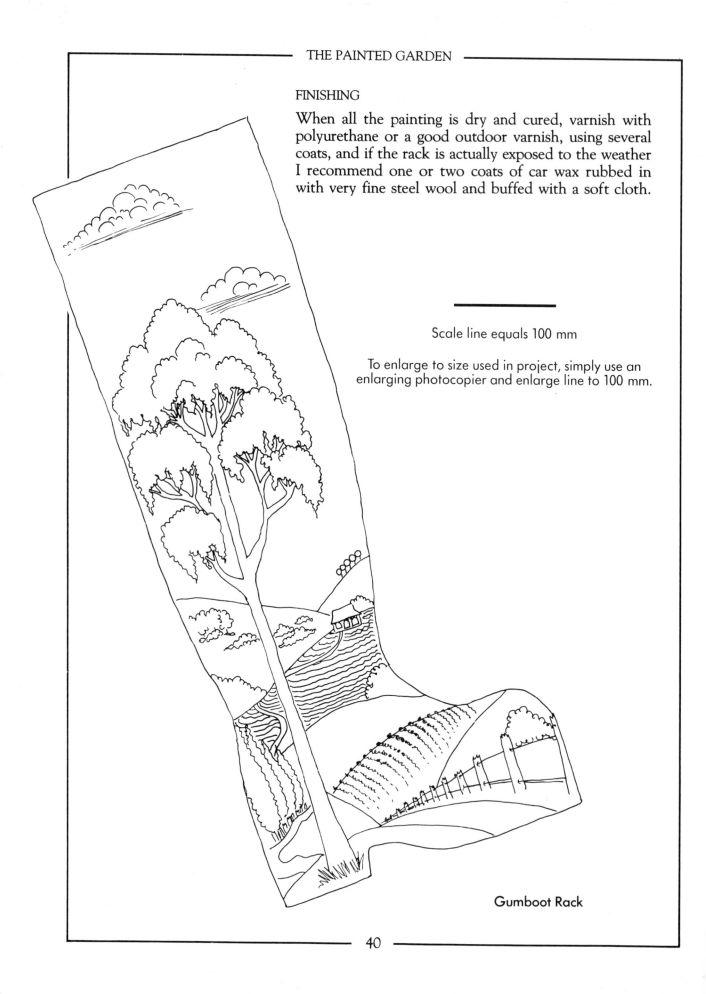

FINISHING

When all the painting is dry and cured, varnish with polyurethane or a good outdoor varnish, using several coats, and if the rack is actually exposed to the weather I recommend one or two coats of car wax rubbed in with very fine steel wool and buffed with a soft cloth.

Scale line equals 100 mm

To enlarge to size used in project, simply use an enlarging photocopier and enlarge line to 100 mm.

Gumboot Rack

WATERING CAN

UMBRELLA STAND

CHURCH BIRD HOUSE

DETAIL OF BACK OF
BIRD HOUSE

BIRD FEEDER

DETAIL OF WHEELBARROW

WHEELBARROW

GUMBOOT RACK

DETAIL OF LEFT-HAND WREATH

DETAIL OF MIDDLE WREATH

GARDENING APRON AND UPRIGHT TERRACOTTA POT

TABLECLOTH AND DIRECTOR'S CHAIR

DETAIL OF TABLECLOTH

HANGING POT AND
WIND CHIMES

GARDENING TOOLS AND GLOVES

THE GARDEN APRON

ABOUT THIS PIECE

I made my apron according to the pattern, out of pre-primed canvas, but I imagine it would work just as well with unbleached calico or a lighter fabric (which might in fact be easier). If you use the unbleached calico, base coat or prime the piece with white or cream mixed with Jo Sonja's Textile Medium. Owing to the fact that I am such a filthy gardener I have included a background preparation for the apron, which is optional. If you wish to paint the wreaths on the apron without any of the brown sponging at the back please feel free to do so, but I knew I was going to get mine dirty so I thought I would anticipate the fact and make it look intentional.

The steps for actually sewing the apron together are as follows:

Having cut out the main part of the apron plus the long strip that forms the three pockets across the front, stitch the folded bias across the top of the apron — that is, the top of the chest of the apron — leaving the edges raw.

Next stitch bias on the top and bottom edge of the strip of pocket fabric. Pin the pocket strip to the body of the apron and stitch in the dividing lines with bias on top of the pocket strip, with the edges turned under both the top and bottom of the strip. Pin the raw edges on the end of the pocket strip to the outer edges of the apron.

Then, using another strip of bias, stitch down the left hand side of the apron (including the pocket strip), around the bottom and up the other side, also catching in the other side of the right hand side of the pocket strip.

Finally, using a strip of bias long enough to include the ties at the back of the apron and the neck strap, stitch the two sides covering the raw edges of the side bias and the piece across the chest.

PALETTE

Red Earth	Warm White	Gold Oxide
Brown Earth	French Blue	Turner's Yellow
Yellow Oxide	Raw Sienna	Burgundy
Teal Green	Green Oxide	Jade
Sapphire	Rose Pink	Fawn

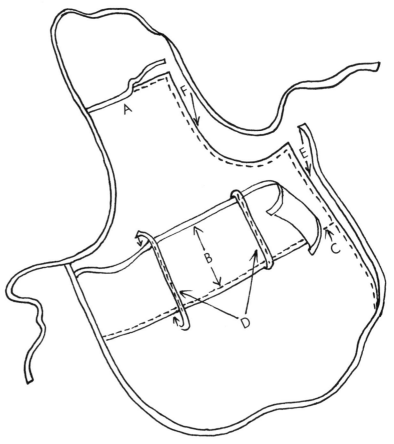

Garden Apron

PREPARATION

After priming the apron with either gesso, or the paint and textile medium mentioned earlier, squeeze out some Brown Earth, some Fawn and some Warm White. With a damp sponge dipped into each of these colours, I sponged a pattern all over the apron and the pockets. You will need a fairly large sponge, or you could use a large brush, although that might make the pattern a little strong. I kept the paint fairly watery so that it didn't show up too dark. Its main purpose is to provide a textured background for the wreaths. You will need to give the apron a few hours to dry, depending on how heavily you have done the sponging. If it is not very wet you will be able to paint on fairly quickly; if you have used a lot of water it will need longer to dry.

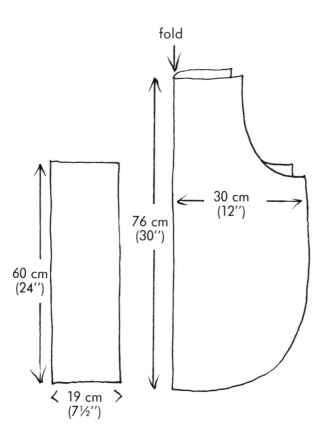

fold

76 cm
(30")

30 cm
(12")

60 cm
(24")

19 cm
(7½")

PROCEDURE

1. **Large Wreath** — Using a dampened sponge and a mixture of Teal Green and Green Oxide, sponge in a circular area where the wreath is supposed to go in the centre of the chest area of the apron. When the sponged area is dry, the next area to paint is the small dark green leaves. Mix a green that is going to stand out from the background and not get lost into it, but not be so violent that it takes all the interest away from the flowers. I took some of the background colours, the Green Oxide and the Teal Green and mixed a little White with them. I then sideloaded again with a touch of White, put each leaf in with a pair of double comma strokes coming to a point, and then went back with the liner brush and outlined them in Teal Green. I then mixed a little Yellow Oxide with the Green Oxide to make the olive green and put in the clusters of smaller leaves that go in amongst the first ones. Once the leaves have been painted, transfer the pattern for the flowers, that

is, the large pink poppies and the cream or yellow paper daisies. The little blue flowers are fillers and you would be better to freehand those in wherever you feel it is necessary. You could put them in on the pattern just as dots, if you wish, and then you would know the basic areas they are to go.

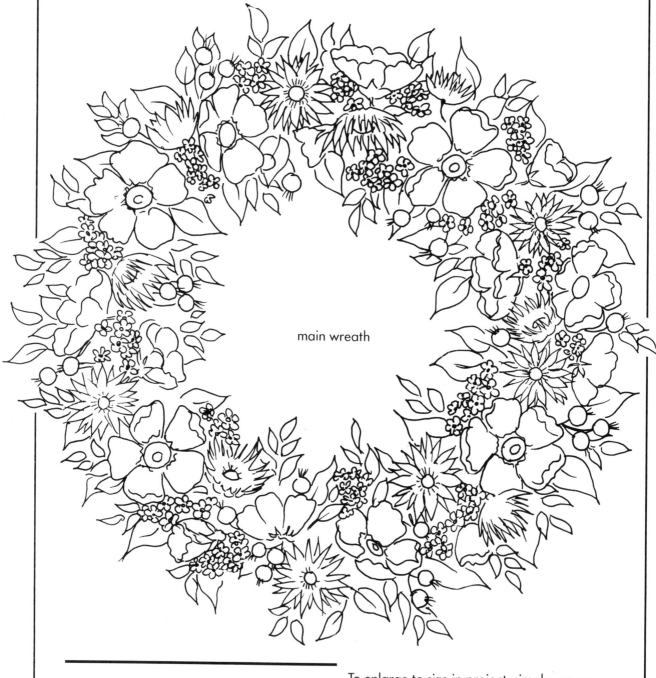

main wreath

Scale line equals 100 mm

To enlarge to size in project, simply use an enlarging photocopier and enlarge line to 100 mm.

2. **Poppies** — Load your favourite round brush with a warm apricot pink, made by mixing Red Earth, Yellow Oxide and a good deal of White. Mix two values of this so you have a darker one for floating the base of the petals, as well as a lighter one for filling in the initial shape of the flower. Using shape-following strokes, paint in each of the petals. Where the petals overlap, you will have to paint it all a flat colour, but try to remember your pattern lines when you go back to put the hightlighting on. These flowers might need two coats of base colour in order to cover the green underneath. Do whatever it takes. When the base colour is dry completely, corner load a flat brush, a No. 6 or 8 will do, with your darker value pink and float a number of U-strokes on the base of the petals where they go into the centre of the flower. Go back to the round brush and load with the base colour pink and sideload with Warm White. Run a white frill around the outer edge of the end of each of the poppy petals. Where you want the petal to flip over, turn the White to the inside of the flower and, starting on the point of the brush, depress down so the White appears to unload as you go across the top of the petal. For the centres, load the round brush with Red Earth and paint a central circle in the middle of all the pink flowers that are fully open and an oval in the flowers that are turned sideways. When this is dry, float a stroke of Brown Earth on one side of each of the centres and put a dab of Raw Sienna or Yellow Oxide in the middle of each flower centre. With the liner brush and some Green Oxide, put the sepals and stems on the base of those flowers that are turned sideways.

3. **Paper Daisies** — I painted these with the large liner brush because it was easier to get the nice long pointed petals. Starting with the liner brush and a deep yellow of Yellow Oxide and Raw Sienna, paint a radiating star for each of the paper daisies. Then load in a little Yellow Oxide mixed with Turner's Yellow to give a slightly brighter yellow and paint another star on top of the first so that a few of the dark petals show, but not all of them, and then add White to that mix and paint the final star-shaped petals on top of the ones you have already painted. Make the strokes long and pointed and all coming from the centre, except where the little flowers are turned sideways to you, in which case you do the

back half first. Put the centre in and paint the front half next, with slightly shorter strokes, coming from the base upwards over the top of the centre. When the petals are dry, paint a small circle of Raw Sienna in the centre of each flower that is facing directly out and an oval of Raw Sienna in the flowers that are turned sideways. Float the edge of these Raw Sienna centres with Brown Earth.

actual size

left hand pocket wreath A

4. **Forget-Me-Nots** — These flowers are the push-dab flowers I use such a lot in most of the patterns. Load your liner brush with Sapphire and sideload in White and push five little petals in a circle in clusters all over the wreath or in the areas indicated on the pattern, whichever you prefer. Each time you place the brush down, if you push the tip of the brush in the same direction you will get a highlight and a contrasting colour on each petal. You will have to keep reloading and some of the flowers will be darker and some will be lighter. It gives a pleasing effect of clustered tiny flowers. When these are dry, add a centre, using a liner brush loaded in Burnt Sienna and sideloaded in Turner's Yellow and another little push-dab stroke in the centre of each circle of five petals. Finally, paint the berries in with straight Burgundy. Allow to dry and, with the liner brush loaded with Black, paint in their stems and the little clusters of hairs that pop out of the top of each of the berries.

5. **Wreath A** — The steps for sponging the background and painting the background leaves on each of the small wreaths A, B and C on the pockets is the same procedure as for the large wreath. The first flowers on Wreath A are bluebells, which are painted with a double-loaded liner brush using a mix of Sapphire and White; the flowers are painted by painting three short fat comma strokes with their fat ends overlapping. Make sure the three comma strokes end up fairly well spaced apart because you need to load the liner brush with a cream mix of Turner's Yellow and White and stroke in the filaments that poke out from between each of the petals. Load a liner brush with a very pale green made by mixing Jade and White and paint in the stems of the bluebells and the sepals attached to the bottom of the flowers as well.

6. **Wreath B** — Proceed to sponge in the background and the two kinds of leaves on the sponged background the same as for the previous wreaths. Using a mix of Rose Pink and a touch of White, paint in the violas that are scattered around the wreath. You have the pattern for this, but I think these flowers are clustered together so tightly you can freehand them on. I did most of them in the Rose Pink variation and the rest of them were in Burgundy. The flowers are just two short, fat, tail-less comma strokes for the top petals and then the bottom petals

are two short, fat, overlapping comma strokes, each coming into the same centre. When they are dry, load the liner brush with Yellow Oxide and paint a number of little short, fine strokes coming out from the centre of each of the flowers. When you have painted the short, fine strokes of yellow in the centre of each of the Rose Pink and Burgundy flowers, load the liner brush with straight Black and paint another little centre over the top of the yellow, with short, fine liner brush strokes. Refer to the picture in the colour pages to check the position of these strokes.

actual size

middle pocket wreath B

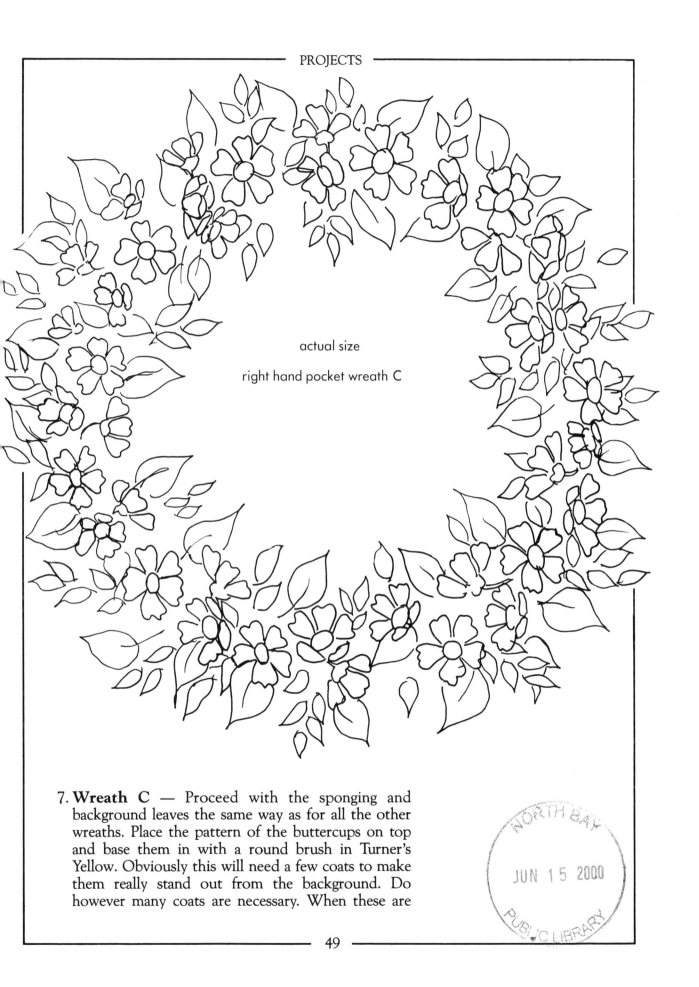

actual size

right hand pocket wreath C

7. **Wreath C** — Proceed with the sponging and background leaves the same way as for all the other wreaths. Place the pattern of the buttercups on top and base them in with a round brush in Turner's Yellow. Obviously this will need a few coats to make them really stand out from the background. Do however many coats are necessary. When these are

dry, outline each petal of each flower with a liner brush and watered down Yellow Oxide. There will be some stems and sepals to put in using pale green. The centres of the buttercups are Burnt Sienna or Red Earth with a semi-circle of stylus dots around one side of each of the centres.

FINISHING

When all the painting is dry and cured, I would recommend giving the apron at least one coat of varnish or your favourite sealer in order to preserve the painting. I was worried with my own apron that this might make it a bit too stiff, but I didn't notice any difference once I had varnished it. I only did one coat, however.

If you wish to, it would be possible to paint all the sections of the apron before you actually stitched the bias binding and the pockets together, although I did make mine completely first.

TERRACOTTA UPRIGHT POT

ABOUT THIS PIECE

There are lots of patterns for painted terracotta pots available, but I was interested in trying this one out, with the painting inside as well as on the rim and less decorative work on the outside. The swag effect also went well, I thought, with the incised lines already on the pot. The only unbreakable rule with terracotta is that you must seal the terracotta first, inside and out, before you do any decorative paining on it, just in case people are going to put moist earth and plants inside. If you know for certain that the pot is going to have a plastic pot put inside it and will only be used for decoration, then sealing is not so important, but if you are going to sell it, then to be on the safe side it should be sealed all over.

PALETTE

Plum Pink	Warm White	Yellow Oxide
Teal Green	Yellow Light	Storm Blue
Black		

PREPARATION

As I have mentioned, sealing any terracotta piece is of prime importance, but with this particular piece I based the inside of the pot in a Teal Green mixed with a touch of Black and some Jo Sonja All Purpose Sealer.

The outside of the pot was first sealed with Jo Sonja All Purpose Sealer as well.

PROCEDURE

1. **Flower Swags** — Draw the outline of the swags around the pot first and base in this area in the same black-green mix that is on the inside of the pot. Then go back with the round brush and, using short, fat, pointed comma strokes, paint in the leaves along the edge of the based area so that you can see half a leaf poking out from the dark area. This gives a foliage profile which is preferable to a straight line. When

this is dry, mix an olive green from Yellow Light and a touch of Black and paint some small leaves in clusters along the outer edge of the swags. It is a good idea to put the pattern of the ribbon on at this time. Using a liner brush loaded in Storm Blue and sideloaded in White, paint the wrapped ribbon around the swags first and then the bows and loops of the ribbon next. Finally, put the rose outlines on the swags so that some of them overlap the ribbons slightly. Check with the step-by-step colour pages on how to do these little roses. They are very simple. First, using a round brush, base in a small circle of background colour, then some smaller semi-circles around that. Change to a flat brush, very small in this case, like a No. 2 or 4, and float a large C-stroke around the base of the circle and a tiny C-stroke where the throat of the rose is. The colours are a very pale pink, which is White with a touch of Plum Pink, and a very pale cream, which is White with a touch of Yellow Oxide. For the floated colour, use the straight Plum Pink and Yellow Oxide.

FINISHING

When all the painting is dry and cured, cover with a coat of sealer or varnish. If the pot is to spend most of its time outside, obviously one coat will not be enough. I usually recommend at least three coats, as well as the car wax application discussed in earlier projects and under Finishing in 'Terms and Techniques of Folk Art'.

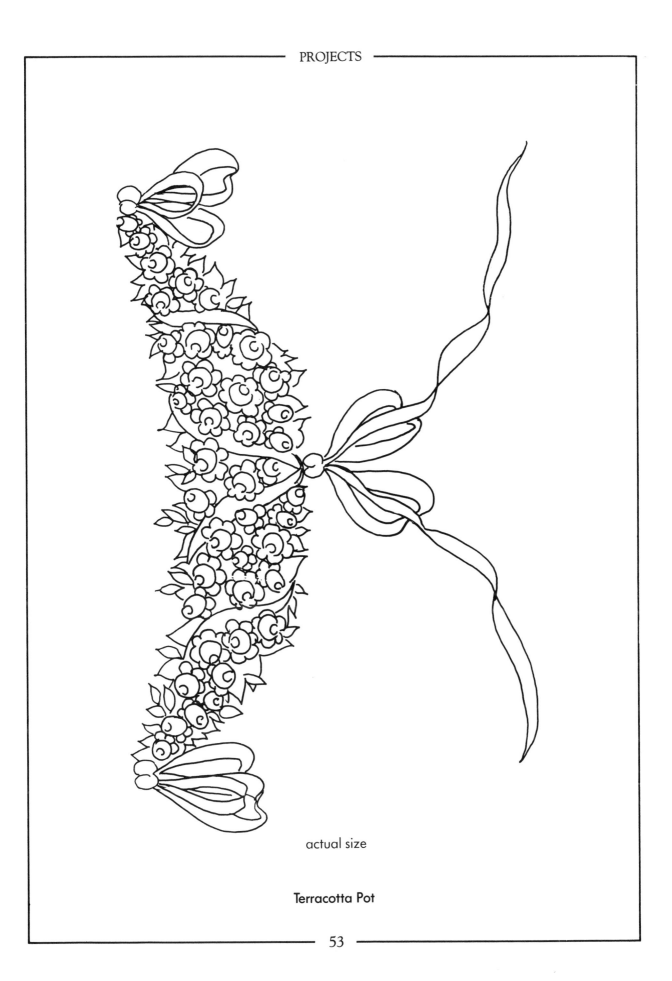

actual size

Terracotta Pot

DIRECTOR'S CHAIR AND TABLECLOTH

ABOUT THIS PIECE

The director's chair was an experiment in painting on canvas and trying to get some fine detail. I don't know that I am entirely satisfied with it, but the effect was quite acceptable. I did not treat the canvas first; it is raw, with the paint straight on top, with a little textile medium mixed into the paint. The tablecloth was made of the same primed canvas as the gardening apron, so it was much easier to paint than the chair because it already had a painted surface. The tablecloth was only painted on the corners, but with hindsight I would probably paint the pattern all the way around. The actual shape of the tablecloth was simply the canvas folded into four with the corners rounded off. The edges of the tablecloth were stitched with the same bias binding I used for the gardening apron.

PALETTE

Gold Oxide
Napthol Crimson
Yellow Oxide
French Blue
Red Earth

Burgundy
Napthol Red Light
Green Oxide
Plum Pink

Turner's Yellow
Warm White
Norwegian Orange
Teal Green

PREPARATION

One item of extra equipment needed for this piece is a fine-tipped technical pen. A waterproofed felt tip might do the job but I am not at all sure. It would be worth some experimentation and of course it would depend on the fabric being used. When applying the pattern with the graphite paper, I found an ordinary stylus on the heavy duty canvas was not successful. The best way to put it on, I found, was having a throw-away design and punching a series of holes through the tracing of the design and a sheet of black graphite onto the canvas. A dressmaker's wheel would work just as well, if not better, and would be less destructive of the graphite and the tracing. This was not a problem with the tablecloth because the fabric was finer. It was only a problem with the very coarse canvas of the director's chair.

Scale line equals 100 mm

To enlarge to size used in project,
enlarge line to 100 mm.

PROCEDURE

1. **Scrolls** — The scrolls on this pattern are based in using Teal Green — more than one coat, if necessary.

2. **Leaves** — For the large leaves, you can chose any variation of the autumn colours of Napthol Crimson, Turner's Yellow or Red Earth. Each leaf is painted in the same way. I painted the outside one colour, that is, the points of the leaves are painted one colour about a third of the way or half the way into the centre of the leaf. The centre of the leaf is then painted a contrasting colour, either lighter or darker, whichever you prefer, although I seem to think the best effects were obtained using a lighter colour in the centre with a darker colour on the tips of the leaves. Then take a medium colour and dry brush over the joins of the two colours you have already put on the leaves. Some combinations that I used were Norwegian Orange and Red Earth with Napthol Crimson in between; and Turner's Yellow and Napthol Crimson with Norwegian Orange in between. Each of these combinations were dry brushed so that they blended as gradually as possible. Painting on the rough surface of the canvas meant dry brushing was the only way to get an effective blend. Some leaves were Turner's Yellow and Green Oxide combinations, as well as Turner's Yellow and Red Earth combinations. If you have trouble with the blending, come back over the middle colour with a touch of the outside colour, or the centre colour — whichever you feel is necessary. The main aim is to get a blending of three colours on most of the big leaves. I usually only use two colours on the smaller leaves.

Chair and Tablecloth

3. **Grapes** — With each of the bunches of grapes, paint a selection (that is, about a third of the grapes showing) in straight French Blue. Then shade those in a darker mix of French Blue and Black. Add a little White to the French Blue to obtain a medium blue, and base in the second third of the grapes of each bunch. Highlight these with French Blue mixed with a little more White.

Finally in this mix, add a little Plum Pink to obtain a mauve and paint the remaining third of the grapes. I highlighted those in straight White. When I say 'highlighted', I mean a dry brush highlight with a round brush — not a float.

Finally, with the technical pen, draw around all the leaves and the scrolls and put the veins in the leaves, and also do all the stems and tendrils with the technical pen. This pattern can be used in units of one or made into a continuous pattern.

FINISHING

I would recommend painting any fabric piece that is going to be left outdoors with sealer in order to preserve the painting. But if you are not going to leave it to the elements, then sealing it is entirely up to you.

HANGING POT AND CHIMES

PALETTE

Green Oxide	Teal Green	Black
Red Earth	Yellow Oxide	Plum Pink
Warm White	Brown Earth	Rich Gold

HANGING POT

PREPARATION AND PROCEDURE

This pot is base coated inside and out with Teal Green. It has flowers and soil inside it, showing no ill effect to the painting after several months, which makes me hopeful of the painting being permanently on the piece. It was, of course, sealed inside and out first. Placing the pattern on this piece is a little difficult because it is curved, however, as it is a continual linear pattern you should be able to fill in the gaps. There are some areas where the pattern will need to be gathered slightly, but if you leave those areas empty, then you can put in what you feel is appropriate with a liner brush. The lines on the pot are Rich Gold, painted with a liner brush, but loaded very heavily so that the ends of the lines can be painted quite fat, as in a comma stroke, but you can still bring it up on the tip and draw in the fine lines. Once the Rich Gold line work is dry, go back into all of the major intersections and paint a cluster of leaves in Green Oxide or olive green made by adding a little Black to Yellow Light. When these are dry, paint one of the small roses in the centre of each cluster. These are based in using the round brush and painting a small circle with semi-circles around it in a pale apricot. Mix this by adding a touch of Red Earth to Warm White. Float a large and small C-stroke for the base and throat of each rose in straight Red Earth. When the painting is dry and cured, seal with the necessary number of coats of varnish.

actual size

Hanging Pot

WIND CHIMES

PREPARATION AND PROCEDURE

These wind chimes are a terracotta piece that I have seen in a lot of nurseries and flower shops and can be used as a mobile as well as wind chimes. The beads are base coated in Brown Earth and the bells are base coated light to dark in the following order: largest is Warm White with a touch of Raw Sienna in it to create a cream; then the next bell down is Warm White with Red Earth to make a terracotta colour; then a little more White in that same mix until finally the last bell is a pale apricot pink. The hearts that are used as the clangers are painted the same selection of colours. The pattern on each piece is the cluster of leaves. This time they are painted in two greens, one cluster in Teal Green and the one on top in Green Oxide. Next add the same little rose I have used on all the terracotta, with some line work around the base of each of the bells. The difference with the line work in this case is that I loaded the liner brush with Brown Earth and then picked up a large portion of Rich Gold and painted the line work so that there is a little bit of extra colour in it.

I intend to hang my chimes outside in the garden, so I am in the process of sealing them very well with several coats of varnish, and will finish them completely with car wax (see Finishing in 'Terms and Techniques of Folk Art').

large wind chime

medium wind chime

small wind chime

Scale line equals 100 mm

To enlarge to size used in project, simply use an enlarging photocopier and enlarge line to 100 mm.

Wind Chimes

GARDENING GLOVES AND TOOLS

ABOUT THIS PIECE

The gloves I used were leather, but plastic would be just as good, or you could paint on fabric as well. The handles of the garden tools were wood, but again plastic could be painted on just as easily.

PALETTE

Plum Pink	Burgundy	Ultramarine
Brown Earth	Sapphire	Warm White
Teal Green	Green Oxide	Jade
Red Earth		

PREPARATION

The gloves did not require any preparation. With the wooden seed dibble I base coated the lower portion of the handle in Brown Earth and I base coated the handles of the trowel and fork in Warm White. Both handles were already varnished, so I sanded them back quite heavily. I didn't take all the varnish off, but gave them a rough surface on which to paint and the paint shows no signs of leaving the handles.

PROCEDURE

Gloves — On the back of each glove I sponged a small area of Green Oxide and Jade mixed together, then based in some round violet leaves on the edges of the sponging, using Green Oxide mixed with a touch of Turner's Yellow to get a more grassy green. Then, with the tip of the round brush, and using tiny comma strokes, I put some clusters of small leaves poking out around the outer edge of each of the circles. Add some White to the original violet-leaf-green and paint in some veins on each of those round leaves.

Violets — Mix some Burgundy with some Ultramarine and paint in a few violets in this very rich deep purple. I only put two or three violets on each glove. It just gives some depth to all the other colours and makes them stand out. My violets are painted with two comma strokes on the top and then a fan of three or four comma strokes on the bottom of the violet. All of these join in the centre of the flower. On the very dark violets, place a float of straight Burgundy on the base of each of the petals where they meet in the centre of the flower. Add a touch of Plum Pink and White to the Ultramarine and make a middle value blue and paint in another series of flowers overlapping the dark violets that have already been painted. These can be floated at the base of the stroke with the first dark violet mix. Add a little more White to this base colour and do another selection of flowers, filling up the spaces as you go. The final coloured violet is a pale pink one, made by mixing Plum Pink and White and floating the base of the petals with the straight Plum Pink. Change to the liner brush and, everywhere you can see a centre of a violet, put two little curved comma strokes. In between these two little yellow strokes put a dot of Red Earth. Finally, with the Warm White and a stylus, dot in some baby's breath in amongst the violets.

actual size

actual size

Garden Tools

Handles — The handles of the trowel, the fork and the dibble are pretty well the same as the gloves, but with a few less leaves. I used the three-greens sponge method on the handles, with the thickest and darkest green being at the base where the wood meets the metal. I did not put any leaves as such behind the violets, but I did give certain of the violets that were standing clear of their neighbours light green stems made by mixing Yellow Oxide and Green Oxide. The violets were painted in the same order, with the deep Ultramarine and Burgundy, then the Ultramarine and Plum Pink and White in two levels and finally the pale pink violets with the Plum Pink floating. All of them have the little yellow whisker strokes and the dot of Red Earth in the centre. They do not have the baby's breath.

FINISHING

With regard to the sealing, I have sealed only the painted sections of the gloves because I was not sure about painting the entire leather area, but I don't anticipate them being a problem to wash or wipe off when they get dirty. The handles had the usual multiple coats of outdoor varnish. The extra coats of car wax as described under Finishing in 'Terms and Techniques of Folk Art' would be useful for these pieces, I am sure.

COLOUR CONVERSION CHART

JO SONJA ARTIST'S COLOURS	MATISSE	DECOART AMERICANA	ILL. BRONZE COUNTRY ACCENT	DELTA CERAMCOAT	FOLK ART
Carbon Black	Black	Ebony Black	Soft Black	Black	Licorice
Provincial Beige	Raw Umber + White	Warm Neutral + Dark Chocolate	Wild Honey + Raw Umber	Territorial Beige	Butter Pecan
Fawn	Ash Pink + Burnt Umber	Mauve	Vic. Mauve + Raw Sienna	Bambi	Chocolate Parfait
Brown Earth	Burnt Umber	Dark Chocolate	Raw Umber	Brown Iron Oxide	Coffee Bean
Jade	Antique Green	Mint Julep Green	Village Green	Leprechaun	Bayberry
Green Oxide	Chromium Green	Leaf Green	Green Olive	Seminole	Fresh Foliage
Pine Green	Hookers Green	Forest Green	Pine Needle Green	Forest Green	Green Meadow
Teal Green	Spruce	Evergreen	Deep Forest Green	Dark Forest Green	Parrot Green
Sapphire	Cobalt Blue + White	True Blue + White	Soldier Blue + White	Liberty Blue	Blue Ribbon
French Blue	Antique Blue	Blueberry	Stoneware Blue	Nightfall	Denim Blue
Storm Blue	Phthalocyanine	Navy Blue	Liberty Blue	Dark Night	Indigo
Ultramarine	Ultramarine Blue	True Blue	Pure Blue	Ultra Blue	Ultramarine
Yellow Light	Cadmium Yellow (Light)	Lemon Yellow	Sunkiss Yellow	Bright Yellow	Sunny Yellow
Turner's Yellow	Yellow Mid	Cadmium	Dijon Gold	Yellow D	School Bus Yellow
Yellow Oxide	Yellow Oxide	Mink Tan	Mustard Seed	Antique Gold	Harvest Gold

JO SONJA ARTIST'S COLOURS	MATISSE	DECOART AMERICANA	ILL. BRONZE COUNTRY ACCENT	DELTA CERAMCOAT	FOLK ART
Raw Sienna	Antique Gold + Burnt Umber	Antique Gold	Tumbleweed	Raw Sienna	English Mustard
Gold Oxide	Terra Cotta	Terracotta	Brick	Terra Cotta	Pumpkin Pie
Napthol Red Light	Napthol Scarlet	Cadmium Red	Jo Sonja Red	Fire Red	Christmas Red
Napthol Crimson	Napthol Crimson	Berry Red	Pure Red	Napthol Crimson	Calico Red
Red Earth	Red Oxide	Georgia Clay	Pennsylvania Clay	Red Iron Oxide	Rusty Nail
Indian Red Oxide	Burnt Sienna + Burgundy	Rookwood Red	Fingerberry	Candy Bar	Chocolate Cherry
Burgundy	Burgundy	Crimson Tide	Bordeaux	Mendocino	Raspberry Wine
Plum Pink	Burgundy + White + Black	Raspberry	Fingerberry Red + White	Dusty Mauve	Raspberry Sherbet
Opal	Ash Pink	Mauve + White	Vic. Mauve + Wild Honey	Misty Mauve	Cotton Candy
Smoked Pearl	Antique Gold + White + Burnt Umber	Sand + White	Off White + Mustard Seed	Sandstone	Tapioca
Warm White	Antique White	Snow White	Off White	Light Ivory	Taffy + White
Titanium White	White	Whitewash	Whitewash	E. White	Wicker White